by Stephen Stepanchev

(poetry)
Three Priests in April
Spring in the Harbor
A Man Running in the Rain

(prose)
American Poetry Since 1945: A Critical Survey

THE MAD

by

STEPHEN

STEPANCHEV

BOMBER

1972
BLACK SPARROW PRESS
LOS ANGELES

ACKNOWLEDGEMENTS

Some of the poems in this book have been published as follows: "The Minotaur," *Antaeus*; "The Tennis Shoes," "The White Lilacs," *Chicago Tribune*; "The Vacation Ends," *Confrontation*; "In Emily's Garden," *Emily Dickinson: Letters from the World*, ed. Marguerite Harris (New York: Corinth Books, 1970); "Things," *Hyn*; "The Empty Bed," "I'm Leaving," "Waiting," *Kayak*; "Like a Woman," "The Mad Bomber," "A Photograph of Che Guevara," *New York Quarterly*; "As The Light Hardens," "Tom," "Three Photographs," *New York Times*; and "The Man in the Window," "The Woman in the Waiting Room," *Works*.

PS
3537
T339
M25

63678

Black Sparrow Press
P.O. Box 25603
Los Angeles, California
90025

LIBRARY OF CONGRESS CATALOGING IN PUBLICATION DATA

Stephanchev, Steven.
  The mad bomber.

  Poems.
  I. Title.
PS3537.T339M25   855'.5'4   72-7485
ISBN 0-87685-123-5
ISBN 0-87685-122-7 (pbk.)

For J.M.

TABLE OF CONTENTS

THE MAD BOMBER

HOME AGAIN

The damp earth floor
Under my bare feet
Quakes

The chair hugs me
Without feeling

I hear iron sounds
Belling the church
Down

I open the shutter
Sunflowers bend their heads

A sigh rises
From the wheatfield

The light boils

ATTACKS OF THE HEART

They said she died of a broken heart.
It was easier then.

Attacks of the heart are not attacks of love —
Unless you can imagine an amorous God
Drawing your lovers up on pulleys of pain,
Up through plateaus of haloes,
Landing in ecstasy in a windless heaven
Where the specialists in agony congregate
With their vinegar sponges.

The heart of light is your pillow.
You lie in the light and change its color to gold.
You will not die of a broken heart,
You dazzling egoist, however much
You chatter about the war that we all lose
In the darkness at the heart of the white light.

IN THE GALLERY

Repetition makes a garden,
But these roses are, clearly, unemployed.
Nature does so much better than this painter
I am expected to admire. My attention
Wanders to a gallery guest whose hair
Is a lair of lights, whose face dreams
Like a wheat field, and whose eyes glisten
With tears induced by her contact lenses.
I mix her in my martini and drink
Her down at the window overlooking the East
River, where the moon is breaking up in shivers.

THE HOUSE

The sun breaks into the box.
Branches stroke the sky.

Hoops spin the waists of the untapped
Girls waiting for harness.

Nerves arrange themselves
Like piano keys.

A vacation on the rocks
Hurries us to the civility
Of organized sound in Maine.

Meanwhile the house breaks
Its locks and windows.
Chairs and cats explode
Through the roof.
The house dances
Drunkenly in the street.

AN EMPTY SHOE

An empty shoe
In the sand and
Footprints leading to the sea:
How melancholy can I be?
Other interpretations are possible.

Things,
Porous and worn rocks,
Act in the shore's
Theater of cruelty.

It isn't that they have all left me.
The rocks keep pressing close.

It is to be one
And no star,
With a heart able to stop,

To see the rock
And the woman's shoe
With the tarnished silver buckle
And the cracks in the leather
Real.

JIMMY

He pole-vaults out of himself
Like a fire.

When he runs through the park
The fog breaks up
And fires blossom on the lake.

When he walks into a room,
Fires carpet the floor.

Shaking hands, he leaves his hand in yours.
Looking at you, he gives away his eyes.
Listening to you, he becomes your twin.

His words leap up
Like a series of little flames.

RAKING LEAVES

It is a Sunday of tweeds and hatted men.
The chimneys are hoarse.
A soot-colored pigeon grips a fence spear.
A squirrel sits up, praying, as it gnaws an acorn.
Birds plunge into cauldrons of flaming trees.

I have torn your letter into little pieces
And am burning them with the leaves
I have just raked.

Dismiss it: conscience is an octopus.
There is a book of reasons.
The whisper of a general becomes a scream
By the time it reaches a private's ear.
Lost in a tank of yesterdays,
I remember that the tent falls apart,
The chair collapses under the fat wish,
Cobwebs veil the piano.

Do a white man's pills
Cure only a white man?

I carry a black sky in my bag.

TURNING

There was an upward thrust,
A green violence of trees.
The nests were singing.
The wind amplified the songs.
The sun, I thought, loved me.
There were lamps in my fingers.
The place knew me.

Now an eye moves in the darkness
Mirroring darkness.
There is a stench of corpses on the rocks,
And the trees are still.
Mist rises from the drains.
Stars cultivate the fields of the dead.
The place does not know me.

IN NIGER

Every grain of sand moves every other.
I am riding a camel over the sands of Niger
While my camel boy walks beside me, barefoot,
In the ghostly rhythm of a Berber caravan.
The camels carry salt bars and goatskins full of water;
They scream under the weight.
There is grass for the camels and tea for me.

I don't remember what I was escaping.
Nothing, after all, is there, and everything,
By which I mean this pain, is here.
My shadow follows me like a dumb spy
Falling all over himself with the facts.
Death is the only retirement from the sun.

The oasis offers no sigh of release.
The palms are leafless,
The water is polluted with ashes and oil.
The camel boy collects dry dung for a fire
And makes me tea at the edge of mirage.
His smile is perfect, but how long will his teeth last?
I sit and wonder at the persistence of mirage.
Who would be willing to buy a pint of my blood?

THE NEW FIRE

Pieces of the night
Disconnect the promise.
The step hesitates on the stairs.
Nakedness stirs the mirror
In the prison of the lie.
She sees the red tongues in the garden
Pasting
The pieces of the day together.
The words may heal
As shadows kneel.
The dream circles the new fire.

WAITING

Waiting for you,
I force the minutes.
Your promise bulges like the ocean.
I think of silk traveling in
The freighters of dead captains.
The stones contract at the door,
And the day falls into a crack
Under my feet.

THE MINOTAUR

White marble columns
In a flaming white light.
A blinding sea.
The light scours the citadel
And the rocks slipping from
Their perch in the cliffside
Where the roots of pink oleander dig
Into rock dust, feeling out
Life on the brink.

Here Aegeus stood waiting for
His son Theseus, threader
Of the maze of Crete, bull-slayer,
Rescuer of maidens,
Straining to see the signal in the harbor,
The white sails.
Here Aegeus saw the black sails
Of defeat and death and, grieving, threw himself
On the rocks below the citadel.

Had Theseus forgotten to hoist white sails,
Or did he count on his father's grief and death?

My own father's face
Grimaces in the void.

The white light fingers through the dizzying
Maze of self,
The home of the minotaur,
The wetness, hunger, and unease of a beast
At the center,
In the darkness,
The boiling darkness.

Shaking, I leave the citadel
And move back toward the dusty roofs
Of the living city.
I touch the white wall where a man is praying
And an old woman is counting onions on a string.

PULLING THE TIDES

Pulling the tides
Must be a drag.
The moon sits
In its bouquet of clouds,
Dreaming of a straight line.

A cat drinks
The moon in the river.

Cold light trickles
Through leaves
And whispers.

A boat breaks
Against black,
Rotting rocks.

The pain keeps talking,
But I'm not put off.

The moon will allow
The sea to inch in.

THE WHITE LILACS

The white lilacs are dead,
The signs of triumph.
The sparrows hurry through their phases,
The hands put on their wrinkled gloves,
The box opens to contain what it must,
The mouth rots.

The wall-eyed pensioners
Sit benched in the park,
Breathing the last dust of their earned deaths.
They dream of a door to a walled
Garden where the sun flowers.
Their hips break;
Their hearts break.

Thieves have ransacked the apartments
Of their souls.

Only a few echoes are left in the corners.

THE WOMAN IN THE WAITING ROOM

The road peeled off, and there she was.
The new leaves spoke of nothing
But themselves as they swung on the branches.
She sat with the cobwebs in a corner
Of the waiting room, I recall.
She spoke with an accent; she wanted "a fire."
Her memories were shut tight, I'm glad to say,
Where no stranger could probe
And magnify
As water distorts a dog's foot.
She said she could love me, and we held hands.
When the train rolled in and by,
She disappeared into the fire that is history.
I remember her because she limped a little.

THREE PHOTOGRAPHS

Her black, surprised eyes
Make a bouquet
Of the veil, the leaves,
The joined hands.

She sits on the rotting stairs
Of love, willing her dream,
A pink purse clutched
In her swollen hands.

Shadows room
In her eyes and knives.
Torn leaves flutter
From her arthritic fists.

IN EMILY'S GARDEN

The light of Amherst falls in stays
Here in her garden. A speckled snake
Coils around a rusty clock.
The trees are all knuckles, knees, and elbows.
There is a famine of reds in all that
Greenery around the pond.

I'd like to see a broken barrel
And wine trickling into a thicket
Of embarrassments. But that's my problem.
Would she have liked a wilderness
Of drunken trees?

I see the candle, the white dress,
The pitcher with forget-me-nots around the rim,
The iron father standing at the top of the stairs,
The sister sitting like a stone angel
At the east gate of Eden.

There was an incompatibility, clearly,
Between her clock and the clocks of Amherst.
Hers was faster, like her heart,
And made its own space.
Does the world exist independently
Of our perception of it?

At the speed of a poem time stands still.
A whisper rises in the leaves: "Oh, damn
The prohibitions! Damn the long alleys
Of ten-pin duties, falls! Damn the dour God
Frowning at the table, his northern noes
Frosting all the windows!

And praise the fast rivers of desire
That move in petals toward bays of light

Where turning selves and vivid contraries
Dissolve in song!"

I take my bourbon and drink to you, Emily,
And to the speckled snake sliding beyond his limits
And to the fat, striped, hairy bee
Crawling all over that dahlia.

THINGS

Things have no metaphysics —
The rain writhes in the dust
And trickles, wordless,
From stone to sewer.

I know what I hate
By what I love,
By absences,
My prison's pin-ups,
The shadow of a hand
Opening a door.

THE TENNIS SHOES

Thunder scatters the song of the bird.
A lover does not wear well, and so here I lie
Under these hostile tulips
At the edge of the Atlantic,
Which keeps foaming and spitting at the land.

Rain walks on the water, and then
The scene empties.

The roots of a tree are
Fingering through my coffin.

I remember only the tennis shoes I laced for her,
Kneeling on the gravel,
When I was twenty.

THE RETURN

The shaggiest poppies grew in the mountains,
Where all points of equal elevation were linked by rain.
Looking down, I could see the dark green forest.
I could admire the calligraphy of the rain
And catch sleet like pearls flung at my cabin windows.
Looking up, I could see sunlit snow in the mountains.
I cried "Om, om, om!" and lost all will and desire.
I became image fragments, tarnishing,
In the consciousness of the few who knew me
Among the burning graves at home.
At first, I might say, it seemed like the answer.

Then the silence got to me. I struck stones
Against each other for company.
I drank poisoned water and ate leper's dishes.

Well, I returned to the horns of horror's tunnels
And recovered my ears. Walking down Eighth Avenue,
I never saw the same face twice, but all were beautiful.
Cars ran over me, but I arose, reborn, and brushed my clothes.

When I saw you standing on the stairs,
Holding a white balloon,
I knew I had made the right choice.
I saw snow in your face and poppies in your hair.
You surrounded me.
You kept talking even while we slept.
Your words dissolved the black door.

ON ANCIENT GROUND

"Only the devil digs graves in the sun,"
She says, driving the archeologist away
With a willow branch: afraid that he might find
The ruins of a temple or a god's broken head
In her rocky acres: afraid of history.
Having lost three sons in the civil war, she lives
By abacus calculations, cooled by
The earthen walls of her hut. A goat bleats
Hungrily above her on the hill.
She waves her green branch at him, laughs, and spits.
She is wearing a yellow kerchief and a black dress.
Soon she sees a bearded, sweating priest walk in
Hatless from the road and crosses herself.
"Only the devil walks hatless in the sun," she shouts,
Retreating into shadow like the torch of a tulip,
Back, back with him, out of the horrors of the light.

THE DAY DISSOLVES

The sheep among the rocks are rocks.
Steam rises from the rocks.
The sun rusts in the water.

Crabs retreat from shadow.
There is thunder in the shadow.
Sea anemones shudder.

A sigh crosses the bay.
A guitar whines.
The day dissolves.

A PHOTOGRAPH OF CHE GUEVARA

They made him kneel
In what he was.
They cut his fingers off
To take his finger prints.

Now the flies quarrel
Over his blood
In the yellow half-light
Of the swinging lamp.

THE BEES OF THE SUN

The hive of the sun
Releases
Its bees
In the cemetery wind
Over unsolved puzzles
Of graves,
Dead women,
Seeds rattling in pods.

You saved me once,
A fire
In a cradle.
Now there are ashes
On my tongue.

The flower I leave you
Has ended its song.

A spider descends
A leaf of shadow.

Who will save me now?

GABRIELA

She lived in an unlit house
Surrounded by man-tall weeds.
Children ran past on the way from school.
She was the mistress of shadows.

She rubbed garlic over the door
And spilled bat's blood and
Graveyard dust on the floor.
She plunged gold-plated sewing
Needles into a male rag doll
Seated before the flaking mirror
Where she cursed, rolling her eyes.

Once she focused her camera
On *him*, secretly, through the window,
As he walked by. "I've got him!"
She cried, laughing. "I've caught his soul."

He was the Evil One, her Arch-Enemy,
The man she had loved under a moonlit cherry tree.

BUYING LILIES

The sky walks into the florist's shop.
Lilies, lilacs, and tulips sing at the door.
Flames of soprano voices leap in the new light.
The owner smiles and offers me an Eden.

Drawn, I resist. Ten dollars is the price of lilies.
My mother fed a family of four
During the Depression on ten dollars a week.

But the green morning whispers like champagne.
I buy the trumpeting lilies and let them cry
In the blue vase on my white, corner book-case.

Now their scent mixes with the smell of sneakers,
Sweat-stained sweaters, and suppers of soup and bread.

THE HURT DAUGHTER

She sits like a clock at the kitchen window
And sees a gnawed, blue-rinsed sky.
In the low west the sun glows like a cigarette
In a carelessly rouged face.
Stomach acid is eating the city.

Someone is playing a piano down the hall,
And someone is weeping.
The red door is shut tight,
But mouths open in the walls.
The gold wallpaper glows in the blue light.

Tina, the hurt daughter, holds her hand
And laughs at a mouse peering from a hole.
Her eyes are storm-wide and black:
The kitchen drowns in them,
The world drowns in their surprise.
No plank or rose floats in that black sea.

IRONDALE

They work in an iron mill
And serve an iron machine.
They stir, they tap the cauldrons
Making rivers of steel.
They melt down in that steel;
Their burning lives melt down.

They soon forget the green
Village of green dances
Leaping on berry hills.
They soon forget the leaves,
Lambs, and falconry,
Father's green history.

At night they pour the slag
Down a hill of slag,
Brushing the sky with fire.
Dozens of cars on the road
Pause to watch their lives
Pouring out like gold.

THE MAN IN THE WINDOW

The man in the window has done
The usual amount of killing.
He smokes grass and giggles,
Watering his pots of pink geraniums
On the yellow fire escape
Down which he can never escape
The fire that he is,
The spontaneous combustion
That is his history,
Ashes,
A name on a stone streaked with white pigeon shit.

Living on an island, he keeps hearing the ocean.
It whispers. He can hear it in the traffic and the trees.

But the ocean will not save him,
And he knows it.
Nothing will.

The spider in his head keeps stitching —
Spitting —
Its web.

Then it goes up in flames.

A BARGE

The black barge throbs as it dredges the river.
Someone has finally jumped out of himself.

There are, also, fire escapes
For lives on fire.

Sometimes a fox gnaws his foot off
To get out of a trap.

But you, Eve:

Eyes of stone,
You see nothing.
Child of sorrows,
Your bones will melt into the prairie,
Your fingerprints,
Your voiceprints blur.

Let me touch you.
The river has no hands.

MOVING OUT

I have missed my train
(I keep missing my trains)
And am sitting on the railroad platform
With my bags,
The furniture of my life,
Which I carry from box to box.
The boxes are getting smaller.

Thunder. If God speaks in thunder,
It is a language no one understands,
Though the tone is unmistakable.

Inscrutable.
There is inscrutable writing on my palm,
Like lightning.
Guilty, your honor.

Ellen comes out of the station carrying her baby,
Which she promptly hands to me.
"Isn't he beautiful?" she asks.
Surprised, I look down at a puffed face and gray eyes.
"Yes, isn't he?" I say in confusion.
He glances at me and goes on — singlemindedly, selfishly —
Constructing his categories.

Moving out, I keep meeting someone moving in.

The train to Chicago blunders in,
Like a tongue in pain.

VOYAGE

I stand on the wharf,
Waving the smoke
Of good-bye away.
Something distorts the scene.

You carry tons of baggage,
Your life,
To Romania.
Will the ship hold up?

A horn warns me
That this pain
Is some sort of punishment.

O Olga,
I am the smoke
Of an old fire
My father's match lit
In a darkness
That is with me still.

Love me, love me!

A horn warns me
There is more than glass
Between us
That we never touch.

My handkerchief
Pulls me
Back to the city.

A truck stands on the road,
Abandoned,
Its motor running.

THE ROADS

As night creates the sun, silence
Shapes whatever you say
Into song. The children run by,
Two by two, making a frieze.

There is a passage of shadow over the iron
Fence and a volley of wind in the yard.
The children are fishing with balloons for stars.
They carry a box of stars.

On the lake more stars are surfacing,
And I make my water-walk.

I will give you all of my roads.

MONDAY

A slate sky.
The windows open
On solid geometry.

My car radio blurts
A disjointed song,
A fractured jazz.

Three private gyroscopes
Keep the car moving
Toward a pale green house.

The house is locked and chained,
But night enters it,
Nevertheless.

On the table
The last daisy is ending its song.
The song is dressed in black.

The fortune cookie said,
"Do not despair,
For you will be happy."

Timed for life
In a strange woman's dark,
My heart keeps delivering
Its death blows.

THE BLIND BLACK MAN

The blind black man does not see his shadow
As the white cane taps on the sunlit pavement.
He is angry at the pity of pedestrians
Who offer to help him across the street.
"Let go of my arm!"

The blind black man knows the sun only
As heat on his eyelids.
He can never know the semaphore of love.
When it comes, it comes as a voice, a word,
A touch as if by braille,
And its betrayals are a blackness
Blacker than blindness.

The blind black man takes the Fall of Man
With equanimity, at last,
But stumbles over a pebble under his shoe
On the shore of an ocean he can only hear.
The break of sunlight on the water
 Is always something else, a matter of hearsay.

I'M LEAVING

When I awoke, a fire blocked the door.
When I ran down the stairs, a cop took my fingerprints.

I have planted all my cries and expect no harvest.
I have buried all my coffins and expect no resurrection.
I have ground all my words to powder and blown them away.

I'm leaving without the promises,
The tarnished knives.

I may return some day
With the voice of a falling sky
And the ticking moon in my bag.

SILENCE

The old woman is no witch, but she hangs
Like a vapor over the street where the boys are bouncing
Balls. Sighs like puffs of low clouds rise from the November
Sidewalks. Wishes stand in line, waiting
To be driven. The boys are risks for mothers
And computers, but she likes their bones, firm
Rumps, and quick hands "to make some woman happy."
It's the repetitions she remarks, the old
Games played by new feet, Nijinsky's faun
Danced by Barishnikov, all still produced
By the angular God in the snow precincts.
The boys play time's clichés like discoveries,
And she sips her tea, content. Shrugging off
The explosions, she delights in the music
Of the boys' voices even as darkness snows
And silence seeps into her ears like an acid.

THE DEATH OF A MILITANT

November withdraws like a junkie.
The gardens are full of ashes.
The walls contract and creak.

The hearse is well-oiled, silent,
Ball-bearing silent as it slides by.

The diggers dig past roots,
Broken glass jars, fragments of brick,
Tile, and flower pots
To make him a grave.

I can see him seething,
Foaming.
He could not believe
That injustice is endemic,
That after millions of words
And years on picket lines
He could lose and die.

The sun hisses
As it sinks into the Pacific.

His friends are tossing pennies on his grave.

LIKE A WOMAN

Terror and desire color the subterranean rooms
Where paranoia cooks its stews.
Close your eyes, and the fern disappears.
Close your eyes, and your kingdom sinks through paper.

Open your eyes. You see the snows of the Andes.
Open your eyes. You see the green shelves of the sea.

Weeds and daisies grow in the garden,
Bees that like blue flowers best,
Raffish bachelor's buttons,
Sweet Williams underlining the path.
The gardener is not dead: he is pruning
The roses with clicking shears.

The man who sees the garden owns it.

Open your eyes: recover your kingdom.
You need not enter the light.
Open your eyes. It surrounds you like a woman.

GOOD-BYE!

Moving from shack to shack,
We have always lived in someone else's
Idea of a house, the cast-off
Walls of tomato farmers, like us.

Having sold the farm, at last, Betty and I
Stand looking at the warped boards, the falling
Porch, the white wagon wheel in the yard,
The stiff grass picketing the frozen roses.

There is nothing here we would rather keep —
Not, certainly, the deaths, the debts,
The disenchantments with weather and our neighbors —
And so we move calmly down the stairs

And get into the car and promise each other
Never to come back, never to think of it,
Even if, somewhere, a moon reminds us of the moon
That smiled at our love-making through the north window.

NOON

Morning was a green water in the leaves.
Noon was a whiskey.

They drank and moved
Underground with the shadows.

A wisp of smoke is
Left in the glasses.

THE SNOW MAN

"You can't force people into paradise.
It tears us apart.
The bomb inside us
Tears us apart."

He stamps his feet on the frozen road.
He stamps in the breath that balloons
From a crowd of pedestrians.
He can't admire the pointilliste
Painting of the snow fall.
He curses the snow man.

The snow man shakes
The dice in his eyes.

GALLIO

I took the ferry-boat from Attica to Corinth
And then the sea-road
To the tribune where St. Paul preached
To the bloody Roman consul Gallio in 51 A.D.
I heard water running under
The cracked columns and fallen roofs.

Later, I sat at a table in an inn
And looked out through the window
Into the courtyard where an old woman in a black dress
Sat singing to herself
Over a glass of wine.

Her song was a patch of sunlight
In that dark, broken landscape.

I fell asleep, listening,
And when I awoke the singer was gone.
Moonlight fell on the thick dust around me,
And weeds grew from the cracks in the floor.
Soldiers with torches came to the door and shouted,
"Gallio! Gallio!"

WHITE WATER

White water moves in the pond.
A steaming horse waits at the rim.
A mockingbird balances on a high wire.
Its song runs like water.

The horse drinks the white
Water and runs into the shadow.
The bird stops singing and
Flies into the shadow.
The pond drains away into the shadow.

A perturbation of the orbits
Of planets
Signals an unseen power.

The key turning in the lock
Of a man's mind
Opens the door to shadow.

THE EMPTY BED

It is adaptation to a hostile environment
That colors the eye
Burning a hole in the fog.
It scatters shadows down the street
As pain plows the serenity of the roofs.
Your bed is empty.
I drop the key
Where you may find it.

AFTER A RAIN

Electricity spurts and crackles
Over the forest of green clouds.
It is a landscape for itching feet.
My dog pulls me on a leash,
And I sniff everywhere
The lives bursting out of the earth.

Out of me,
Out of me,
I give them my skin to tent in.
It is large enough for the mole
And large enough for the hawk
And large enough for the light
That lives in this echo.

STAND

The boats go up and down and are happy in the water.
My aunt points them out with her parasol,
And I consider how the sea could contribute its motion
To whatever one might be doing.

Gingko trees grow along the shore,
Green as the gestures of George Washington
In his little park surrounded by black pickets.

Two boys worry a girl with whistles
And bicycle into a grove I know
Where there is a smell of brine.

The smell of gasoline
Overcomes the odor of violets I am carrying
In a paper cornucopia.

"I have spent a day with you
And my hair is still brown,"
My aunt says crossly.

Sunlight falls, my aphrodisiac,
And I leave abruptly.

In winter, of course, the gulls slide as they land
On the ice and scream, ruffling their feathers.
When the ice cracks under their feet
They can see the liquid interior
And a wide-eyed fish or two.

LOVE POEM

This night extinguishes the white page
On the sidewalk
The snow of sunlight
The lamps in the houses
In the mind
The band of beads in your hair
Your hair

This night circulates on the roads
Ignoring signs
In my veins
Pumping with my pump

This night fills your shoes
The blood on your hands is black
I'm embarrassed to say
In this widening universe of night
Where a black wind
Blows the stars out
I love you

ACCIDENT

Her brown eyes stayed a little longer,
Prints in the air.
There was a panic of broken glass.
My feet were bleeding.

I stepped off the curb
Into a pond of stars
Orbiting around my head,
Where the ghosts are.

Traces in my shambling,
Salt in my bread,
Her idea lives in me.
Brute change is dead.

ONE

The roads
Meet in his hand.
He is buried in me
As I am buried in him.
He stands in my shadow.
He assembles and disassembles my heart.
He colors and bleaches my blood.
He enters my dream.

In this fast river
I see, as in a mirror,
The face the wind makes.

I wash my freckled hands.
I wash my freckled mind.

As winter diminishes the elm,
I become as perfect
And inexhaustible
As an angel
Or a rock.

THE PUDDLE

A rough mirror,
I'm grounded in mud.
I'm indifferent to my raw edges,
My reputation among women.

Elementary in my humor, I splash
Your stockings and laugh as you
Raise your skirt and jump.
I see Valhalla.

I'm afraid of the night that dims
My mirror and frosts my shores with stars.
I'm afraid of the sun that lifts me
Out of myself and shrinks my shores.

I like the rain that drowns my thinking
And widens me into a sea.

THE MORAL LIFE

To open the door
Is a kind of morality.
I shudder.
I see
Choices
Leading to
A massacre of innocents.
Dice scatter the heart
In a million
Daily murders.

THE MAD BOMBER

You don't read me,
And so I keep rustling like an old sign.

Yesterday I poured gasoline all over myself
And flamed like a monk
To move you.
You passed by without even calling
An ambulance.

I'll picket you.
I'll carry a placard saying "Unfair to Me."
You mad bomber,
Stop dynamiting those banks and
Come to bed with me.

Must your nakedness carry a political message?
Must you proselytize even during an orgasm?
Where have you been all night,
And why are you leaving the house?

I keep translating my simplicities
Into complexities that you can understand.

Pour the ocean
Into this glass.

THE TIP

I sit on a gravestone
In a lily-pad
Of shadow.

Like someone risen from the dead,
I'm hungry and eat boiled eggs.

I have come, as they say,
A long way.

A gust of wind rushes
Through the tree above me
Like escaping steam
And amplifies the shadow.

I shiver.

A yellow butterfly alights
On my horn-handled, steel knife.
I see, for the first time, a gold knob
On the tip
Of each of his black antennae.

COUSIN

The Atlantic hits steaming rocks,
And the light foams in the water.
Living on an island, I can always hear the water.

There is a trace of darkness in the light,
Like arsenic in the water.
The afternoon melts,
And shadows lurk in the basements of the self.
Shadows expand into night
As pools expand into the ocean.

I'm not surprised you are afraid of me;
I'm afraid of myself.
There is a room inside me where a cousin no one knows,
Hidden and appalling, lives.

He lives in boiling darkness.

As I look at you,
He opens his eyes wider.

CUT WRISTS

This is a winter of absences.
A large death surrounds a little life,
A stump of cabbage in a field of snow.
Cornstalks rustle as the snow falls.

I walk along the Sound where weeds
And questions grow among the rocks.
The sea is shaking out her skirts.
She is indifferent to my cut wrists.
The boats that sail her are as silken as sighs.

A WIFE

Once you were afraid of shadow.

Soon enough the little beds
Accumulated like the effects
Of illusion that they were, and
Questions spread like prairie fires.

I came through the wood
And saw the light fall
Through the trees
And saw you bending
Over the lake and washing
Your hands.

The level of the lake was falling,
And the island you owned
Was no longer an island.

You could live with shadows at last.

OAK

The oak tree does not walk around
The park for another view or run to see
Where the firetruck is hoisting its ladders.

It must be deeper than I think,
This concentration on place,
Where the soil acids are familiar.

Whatever arrives stays put, like a nest
Or a kite grounded in the branches.
Rain and fog are welcome disturbances.

The sun hisses in the leaves,
Making a tent of green light
And recalling the scarred tourist

From his dream of places to the
Cinders and sweet waters of the root.

REMEMBERING AUDREY

Sitting on iron stairs,
Confessing,
Fingering each other's scars,
We lived like the house
That carried our address.
It was often on fire.
Once I found my brother's shoes
Under your bed,
And I stepped into the crack
That tears worlds apart.
I forgave you long ago.
Now there are ashes on my tongue
And ashes in my hair.
I still love you, wherever you are.
My bed will always be your address.

THE MOTORCYCLIST

The motorcyclist thunders in
On silver and leather,
Asks for water, and disappears
In a series of explosions.

She watches him go
And sprinkles water on the dust.
Her eyes are bleeding.

DREAM

We sat beneath the parabola,
A vaguely phallic, decorative palm,
And watched the sun nibbling at the sea
And drank iced coffee with lemon peel.
"Reality consists of echoes, resonances,"
My friend said. "The life of particles
Inside the atom is like a game of pool."
Slightly out of focus, a band of bony children
Broke into the hotel, set it on fire,
And came out eating steak and cream puffs.
"Parallels are fascinating," my friend said.
"A metaphor may be more than a play of mind
Leading to a perception. It may, indeed,
Be the point at which all parallels meet."
The children jumped over the stone wall, tore
The beach umbrella, overturned the chairs,
And pissed into the pitcher of lemonade.
"Reality may also be a series of contrasts,
Tensions of opposites," I said uneasily.
The children sat around us and grinned
With broken teeth, smacking their lips, as we drank
Our coffee. "Not at all — a contrast is
A form of resonance, really," my friend said
As we leaped, satyr-like, along the sea-rocks,
Chased by the children.

PENSIONER

Putting up a curtain in the room
That became his destiny,
He saw the night climbing up the window
And dissolved into the things around him:
They found cups, pipes, and copper wire in the box
Of his brown look, the color of the walls.

INCIDENT

Belching beer, men weave past the red
And yellow neons of this bedroom suburb
Where fake comets and stars dance to the rock
Of the Rockaway Explosion.
Snakes of light travel the railroad track.
A jet screams, rocketing over roofs.
A dog crosses the street like a soldier under fire.

My blue footsteps hesitate on the viaduct.
Fog billows out of the shadows.
A girl with wet hair turns and stares at me.
There is blood on her face, and I stop to speak,
Thinking of my own scars.
Touching my arm, she turns and runs away.

LOOT

It is not the love of shadow.
The purpose of dying, if it has one, is to forget
Unease, the speaking of water,
The lives of bats in lightless caves
Among feces that smell like hydrochloric acid.

My father never went to the movies,
And he was rough on animals.
But he liked to make things grow,
And the house was full of feathery ferns.

When I returned from his funeral,
I found the house had been ransacked.
The mattresses were overturned;
The drawers gaped.
I walked over buttons, shirts, and underwear.

What madman had supposed
He would find an old man's hidden treasure?

His will to remember had been draining for many years,
And shadows had stolen his love of green.
There was nothing left to steal.

SEPTEMBER

New rain spits in the old puddles
Of sick September.
A road wavers beside me,
And the dynamo of distance hums.
A dove mourns in the aspen,
And a pig surrenders to the knife.

THE LAKE

The mental hospital launched its boats there.
The lake was banked with iris and clover
Where promiscuous bees hovered and buzzed.
There, as the nights cooled, my dog
Would lose himself in scents.
Sunken lights glowed in the water.
The corpse of a slain lover rose
In the bell-buoy's praying.

Now the lake has been drained,
The boats are unroped,
The restless bell-buoy is at rest.
The blue fish keep flopping in the mud.
There is nothing much to see, no lover, no sunken light,
Transmogrifications of madness in the processed night.

WOMEN

It is not only in New Guinea,
Where irises are sacred,
That "women are dangerous."
Blowing Venetian glass vases
Or clocking poppies in Turkey
Or rolling like a wolf in the scent
Of a mule to pick up his track,
The new woman can inspire terror.
Men depreciate in value like a car.
They know fractures deep in their engines.
They erode into distances
And deserts like erasures.

On the other hand, you can't keep
A good woman down.
Bleeding like the light on these stones,
I remember a ditch full of goldenrod
In my aching school days
When my father shot a beer can off
The head of my brother John
And said, speaking of my mother,
"I could fall in love only with a woman
Like her,
A woman who could kill me."

THE WHITE FOG

With the bravery of the boated,
I slide by the bell-buoy anchored
In waves whose movement activates
Random alarms over the channel's rocks.
Triangular, rusty, and mindless,
It is nothing but a slow clock, like my heart.
A fat sea-gull rests on it
And grumbles as I float by.

Later, in my green plot on the Sound,
Where, like a hippopotamus,
I rot in the mudhole of indolence,
I hear it in the depths of my bourbon sleep.
I hear it in my pulse and awake
At six o'clock to find that the world
Has rocked into a white, immeasurable fog.

ACROSS THE SNOW

I walk across the snow
Toward the mountain.
My shadow walks beside me
And shivers
Until I reach the mountain
And my shadow
Joins the great shadow.

DEATHBED

She felt that the night was humiliating
Her with order in a collapsing scene
Where fire slept in the womb
And the towers of yesterday crumbled
Like versions of the self corroding in shadow,
Bells in a fog.

She was grateful for the morning's difference,
The rolling engine of the sky, the moment's
Bouquet of tulips and corollary state of belief,
A movement toward something like love
As the sun postponed her execution.

THE GIRL IN THE WINDOW

The girl with the scar on her belly
The girl in the window
The girl is laughing
She is laughing his blue eyes
Out of the scar on her belly

He stands in the snow
He wants to paint the snow
He stands in steam
He wants to paint the snow red

Silence crawls between

It is 5:00 p.m.
The blue bus throbs, exhausts
The trip

Steam boils out of the volcano
Black ash rains over the reef
The wind plants flaming birds
Butterflies write messages

He climbs ashore and spits
A girl with a scar on her belly
A girl with a prayer wheel
She is laughing
She whirls the prayer wheel
She carries blue eyes on a tray

THE SHOE

My canoe drifts between cloud
And water. It leaves
Me among lilies

Opening on pads of shadow,
A sawed whiteness,
A silken coffin,
A scented breath.

The mask slips.
Smoke rushes out of my eyes.
The day keeps willing
Another mile.

I don't believe in sacrifice.
My shoe rots
In the green water.

TV EYE

Dead fish, cats, and cars
Seed the sloping gutters.
A claw is shaking dice.
I run through a lit fog.

Safe in my cave of rejections,
I huddle over a blue eye,
Omniscient and ubiquitous.

The eye creates what it
Measures: the universe and
Its seizures, the short circuits:
War, theft, rape in bending coils.

It is a silver intelligence,
Amoral as rain,
Embracer of opposites,
Master of numbers,

Ticking, humming in paradoxes,
Shadows, regrets of history,
Making the horror it reports.

The eye is I.

THE MIND

Shot through with holes,
The mind is a collection of rooms,
An enchanted foam,
More space than thing.

Or it works on the river
Like a gull, an operative ghost,
Snapping up minnows,

Or, like a fisherman, spreads its nets,
Its filaments,
Collecting mackerel.

The river keeps wandering
As the specialists in agony
Look down from heaven and smile
At the hungry spider in the wind.

THE VACATION ENDS

The road blunders
And smothers in the thicket.
He hears the lake; he sees the green
Cliff, suddenly, as he strides toward the water.
He finds no solace in the lake's watery kiss.
The vacation is ending, and
Nothing was won or lost.

                                       A bird call
Fraternizes with the crack of a gun.
The echo limps as a rabbit reddens and falls.

THE SONG OF THE GUITAR

The lake sleeps.
The windows sleep.
A meadow of stars rolls
Under my boat.
The lake lips it
As I play my guitar.

Vaccinated against it,
I do not want to relive it.
Minutes rain and trees alter.
Jane has told me more
Than I want to know
About her tenth lover.

I play my guitar.
I play for a black bird
In the heart of the lilac
On the careless shore.

Yesterday creeps in,
Wailing,
And an unfriendly hand
Shakes the lake.
The sky empties of stars
And dissolves.
My shadow widens
Into a universe.

Too soon, too soon,
My guitar will hang
On her green wall.
My fingers bleed
In the black wind.

WALKING THE PLANK

Six a.m. insomnia of street lamps.
The sun drinks up the fog
And lights bonfires in the windows.

The train slips in, erasing the platform.
A tunnel gloves and ungloves the train.

Scarred oaks carry the initials of dead lovers.
An axe grins in an oak stump.

A boat rocks in the kisses of the bay.

When I arrive, I find she is not at home.

In the garden
A rose offers scent it cannot smell,
Color it cannot see,
Nectar it cannot taste.
Does it imagine a nose, an eye, a tongue?

A meeting is a miracle, like perfect pitch.

TOM

His iron marriage
Was boated in horror,
The lake raising its fur.

He walked out of the boat
And ignited the midnight
With his singing.

One-eyed as my television set,
He talked about the murders
Of history, but preferred, like Thoreau,
"The news of eternity."

He cracked the truth like a walnut,
With his teeth. He really listened
To the trees. He put his ear to the bark
And felt the anxiety of twigs and leaves.

His death was an easy translation
Into green. I can hear him
Whispering in the weeds.

FIFTY-SIX

Fifty-six.
Fifty-six dry sticks.
My fingers are dry sticks.
The knuckles crack and split
In the flames.

The blue blaze.
Can you see the blaze
In my eyes?
A city is on fire
Behind my eyes.

The white smoke.
Can you see the smoke
Tanning my hams?
No filters catch it.
My love's bellows
Blow up the billows.

Heart?
I have coughed up my heart.

I LIVE WEIGHTLESS

I live weightless
In a room without gravity.
Mad as doors,
The horses of my attention
Laugh. The sun cracks
Open like a melon at the window.
The leaves of minutes flame,
And smoke erupts in the corners.
Ferns slumber in the coals
Where promises once made a garden.

They breathed in unison.

Bits of her still hang in the things
She used, touched, and saw

And in my bleached blue eye.

VETERAN

There is a war of sparrows in the gingko tree.
Clouds are lowering.
The garden speaks in a language of gestures
As the petals of roses disarrange themselves.

He is lying on the grass,
Lost in his day-long
Search and destroy operations
In the free-fire zone inside him.

His shoes fill up with night.
His eyes fill up with blood.
Somewhere inside him
A door tears open
With a word.

There is a bullet of silence
At the center of the word.

FIRST LOVE

Eight o'clock.
The sun withdraws
From the tenant in her eyes,
The bristles that scrub the kiss,
Surprising as the first taste of cotton candy.
The drops are tentative:
A girl trying to control herself.

The pocked pond fills.
Two boys plunge into it
With knees held high, like horses.
The tree of heaven bends
Under the weight of wet leaves,
Green voices,
The appalling bird of the night.

A SEA

I like what you have become.

Unlike the astro-engineering of supercivilizations,
Which brilliantly modifies celestial bodies,
This flawed, human engineering of love
Modifies the look of eye, the break
Of inner waters, after centuries of trying.

I like what you have become in this white fog
As you stand on the rock, eating an orange.
The juice drips on your sweater.
You are bursting with red, black, and lavender
Colors. The water at your feet adds green.

Off in the distance, a crow creaks,
Crowned with volts. Iridescent water
Slides from a waterproof duck.
An ambulance of sparrows carries
The bruised sky.

I, sitting on an old plank, am in motion too.
But my mind stands still,
Like a candle flame,
As I listen to the breathing
Of your sea.

THE EXPLOSION

I stand in the gutter and wait.
The morning risks a little light.

My bag is heavy with
Guts, hearts, and heads.

I have risen from the explosion
With your hand in my hand.

AS THE LIGHT HARDENS

Do wires move me?
There are no wires.

Night breaks into the house,
And the known becomes the unknown.

They have asked me for her old dresses,
And I am cleaning out the closets.

I am cleaning out the closets of despair.
What strange colors, styles, and textures!

I see her sitting on a bridge,
Dangling her bare feet in the river,
Singing of the "subways of the heart."
My own heart is continents away.

Glass prevents the singer from entering,
But the song comes in, nevertheless.

Look. There are moths in these old dresses.

My hands turn yellow
As the light hardens.

Printed September, 1972 in Santa Barbara for the
Black Sparrow Press by Noel Young. Design by
Barbara Martin. This edition is limited to
1000 copies in paper wrappers; 200 hardcover
copies numbered & signed by the poet; & 26
copies handbound in boards by Earle Gray
lettered & signed by the poet.

194

Stephen Stepanchev

Photo by Arun Dhundale

STEPHEN STEPANCHEV received his A.B. and M.A. degrees from the University of Chicago, where he was a scholarship student. In his senior year he was elected to Phi Beta Kappa. He helped to organize the University of Chicago Poetry Club, which was enlivened by the participation of Edouard Roditi, Paul Goodman, and Jean Garrigue. After four years in the U.S. Army, he resumed his graduate studies, but at New York University, from which he received a doctorate in American literature. He teaches at Queens College of the City University of New York.

He has published three collections of poems: *Three Priests in April* (1965, *Spring in the Harbor* (1967), and *A Man Running in the Rain* (1969). His only prose work is *American Poetry Since 1945: A Critical Survey* (1965). His poems have been praised for their vivid imagery, emotional power, and dramatic immediacy.